The Icky Sticky Anteater

Everyone knows that anteaters eat ants, right?
Well, that's almost true. Almost, but not quite . . .

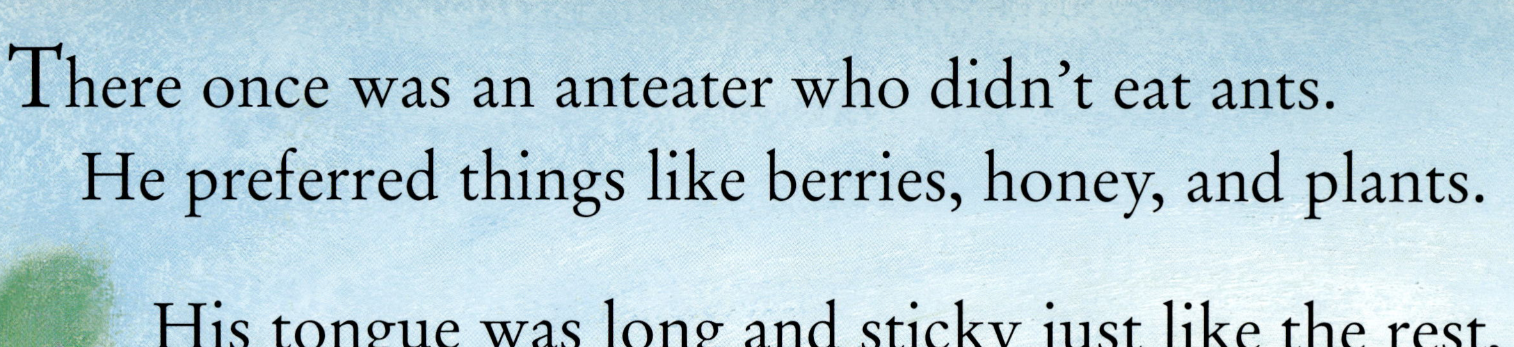

There once was an anteater who didn't eat ants.
He preferred things like berries, honey, and plants.

His tongue was long and sticky just like the rest,
But he found just the thought of ants hard to digest.

The other anteaters shook their heads in disgust.
"Eating ants is your job! And eat them you must!"

So he stuck out his tongue and wrinkled his snout,
And in ANTicipation, began searching about.

As he walked through the grass,
he soon found a hole.
Zip! In went his tongue and
out came a . . .

"What's going on?!" said the sleepy mole, blinking.
"Silly me!" said the anteater. "What was I thinking!"

He found another hole by the shore of the lake.
Zip! In went his tongue and out came a . . .

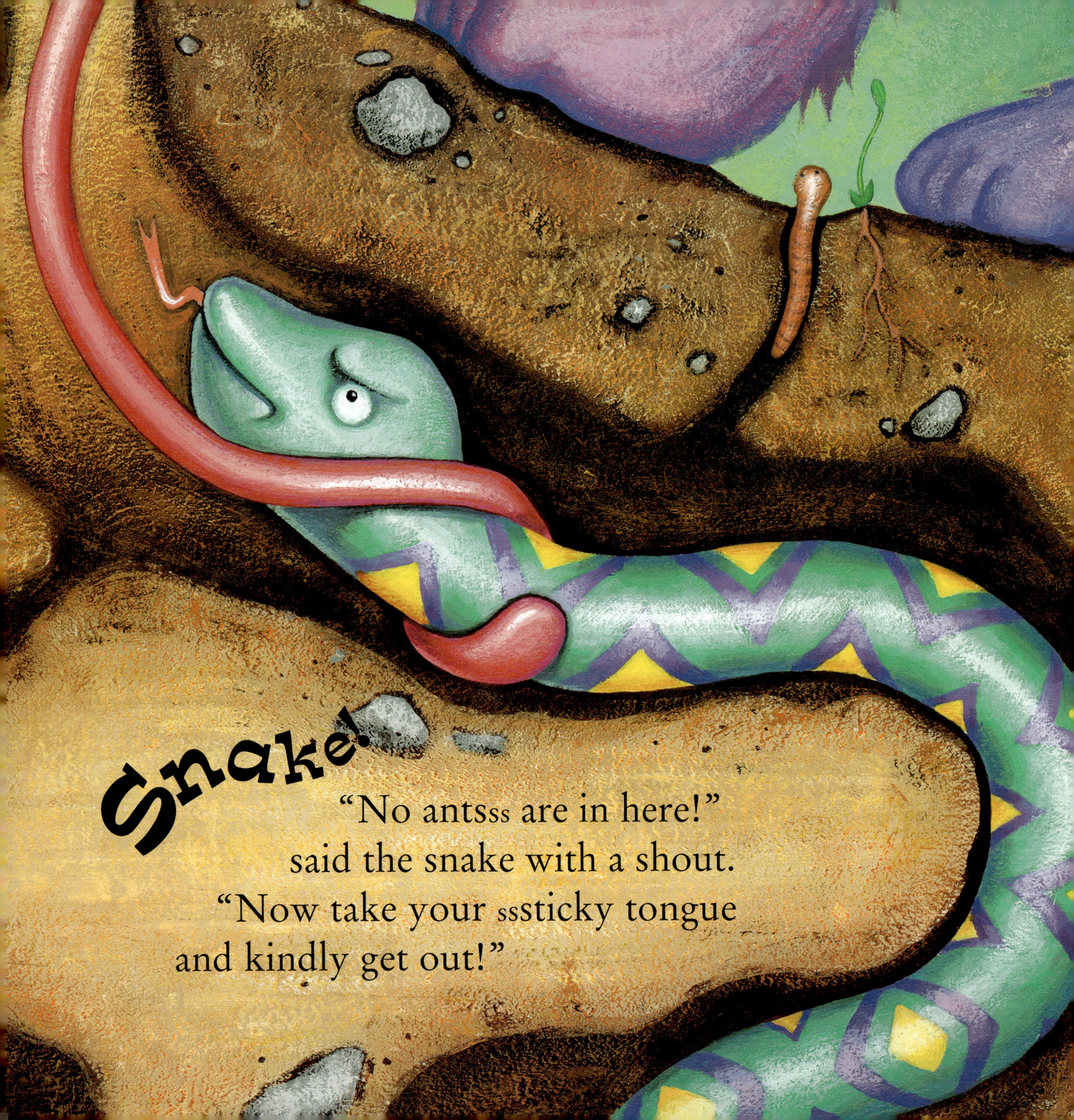

"No antsss are in here!"
said the snake with a shout.
"Now take your ssssticky tongue
and kindly get out!"

He found another hole and quite out of habit,
Zip! In went his tongue and out came a . . .

Rabbit!

"Hey! Stop that!" said the rabbit, hopping mad.
"My mistake!" said the anteater, who was growing quite sad.
"I can't find any ants," he said. "I just can't."
But the next thing he knew, on his tongue was an . . .

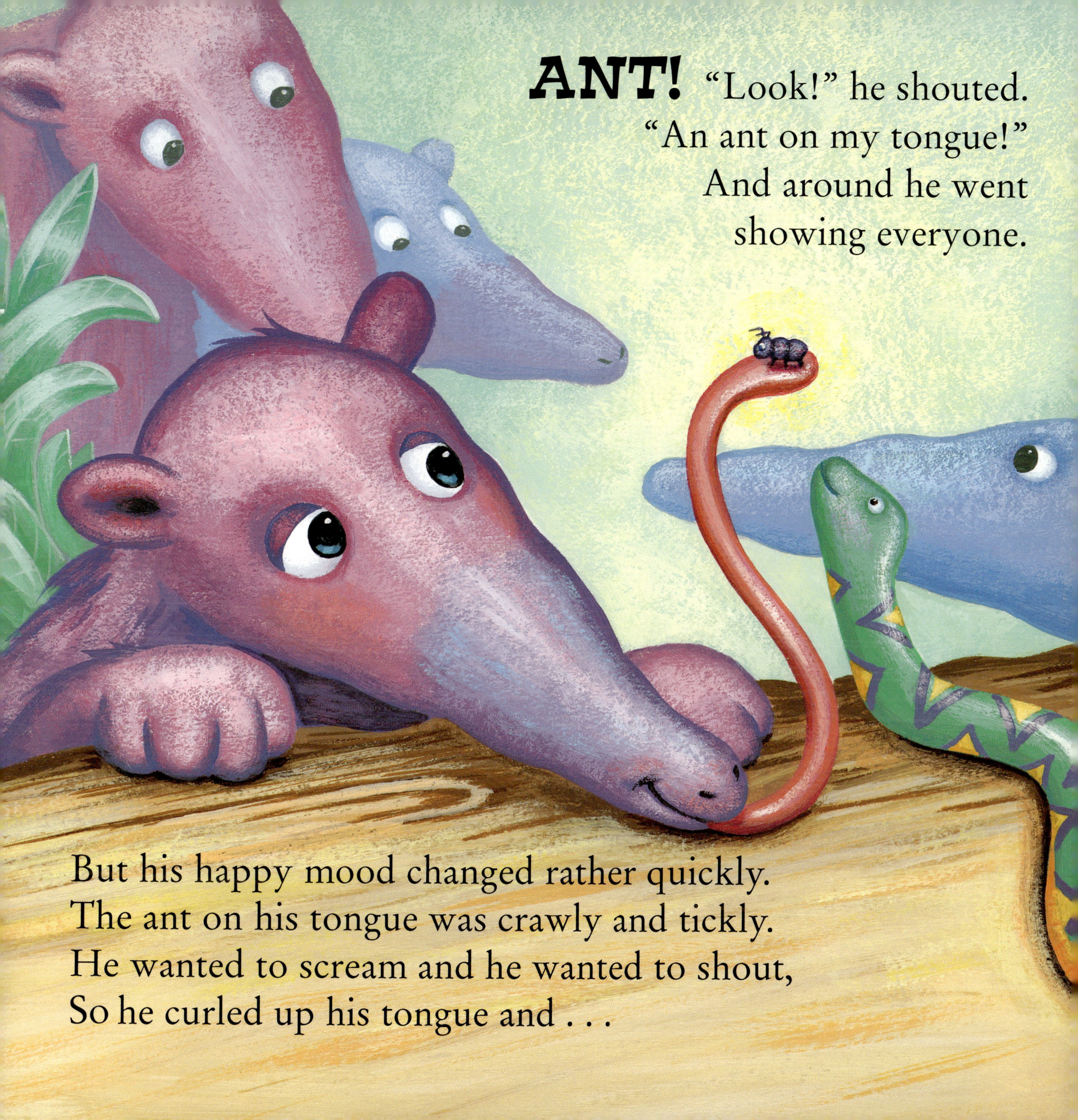

ANT! "Look!" he shouted. "An ant on my tongue!" And around he went showing everyone.

But his happy mood changed rather quickly.
The ant on his tongue was crawly and tickly.
He wanted to scream and he wanted to shout,
So he curled up his tongue and . . .

PHOO! spit the ant out!
"I can't eat this ant! I can't and I shan't!
I'll stick to eating berries, honey and plants!
Everyone is different, that much is true.
I've got to be me and you've got to be you."

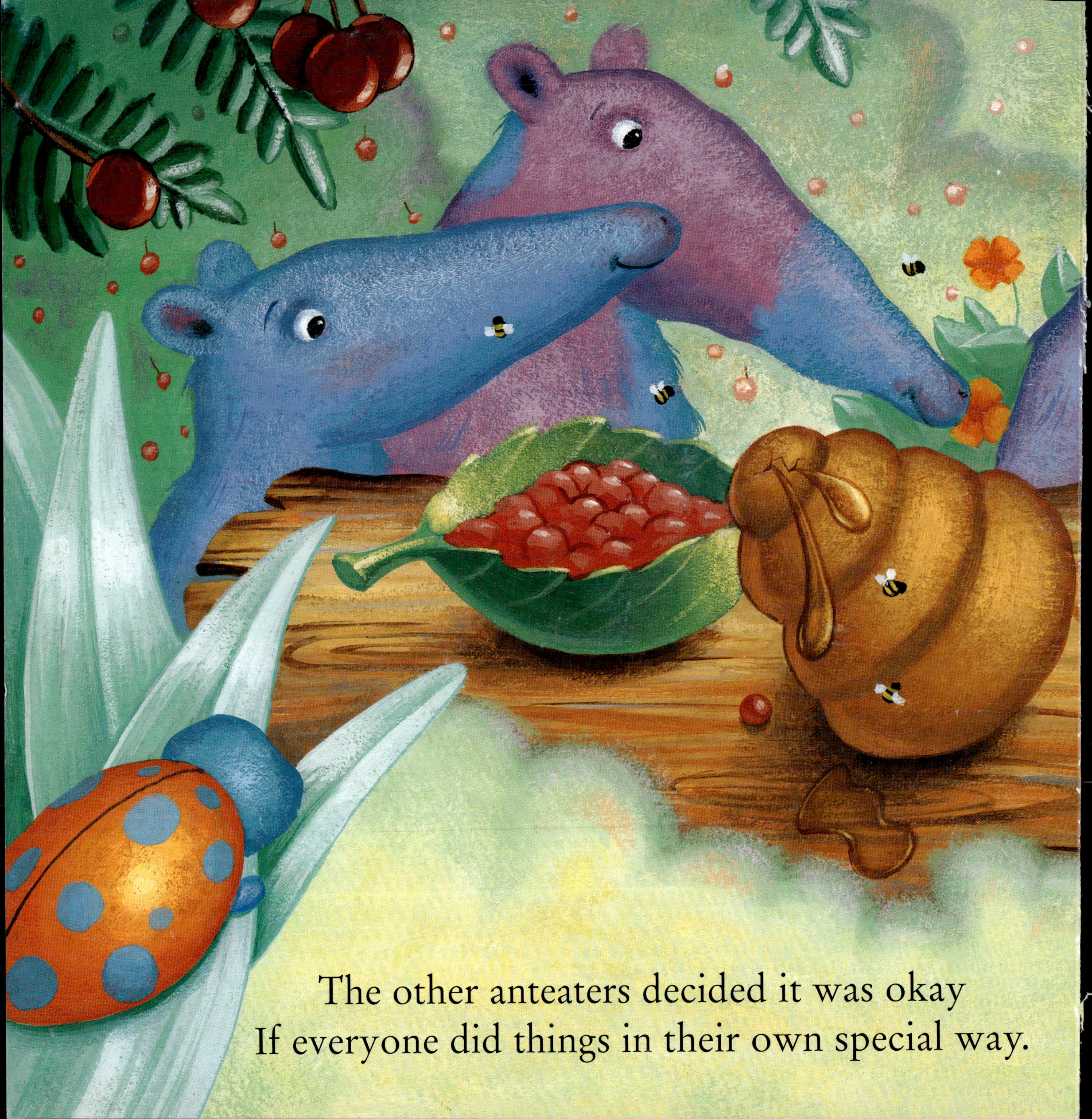

The other anteaters decided it was okay
If everyone did things in their own special way.